Singing Crystals

The Creation of a Crystal-Energy Network

Linda Susannie Boutet

ISBN: 978-0-9938871-0-9

Published by:

A Different Point of View Publishing
Box 2143
Invermere, BC, Canada V0A 1K0

Front cover design: Elizabeth Segstro
Front cover photo: Halgrave Lake, British Columbia

For Gaia

Table of Contents

Introduction

My intention in writing this book is not to re-invent the wheel but to offer clear, concise information on working with power places, sacred circles and crystals. Since the shift on December 21, 2012, our abilities to work with energy have become easier, stronger and more effective. We are being asked to ground Light on Planet Earth and the information presented here is designed to help you to understand one of the ways in which this can be done.

Some of you may be sceptical about working with energy in this way and that's completely OK. It may be that you're not ready for this kind of information yet or maybe you've received this book as a little 'push' from your spirit guides telling you it's time to expand your horizons a bit. It has been my belief for many years that just because science can't prove that energy works in these ways doesn't mean that it doesn't – it just means that science hasn't yet developed the equipment sensitive enough to measure it. If you need proof, start exploring the field of quantum science.

As I was growing up things like telepathy, seeing auras, hands-on healing and distance healing were considered 'woo-woo' by most people. Now, with the discoveries of quantum science, these things can be proven. Our connection is very real and science now supports this. If you would like to know more but you think that quantum science is way too complicated for you, there are many sources that offer simplified explanations. One of my favourites is the DVD *What the Bleep Do We Know*. Or you can do a Google search for Dr. Fred Alan Wolf, aka Dr. Quantum, who has created a series of video cartoon clips that explains many of these discoveries.

In the summer of 2001 I was learning how to use the internet for the first time. I was drawing a total blank about what to type into the address bar until I thought about trying www.lightworker.com. I had learned about Lightworkers from the work of Lee Carroll and Kryon, whose information I had been following since 1995. I was surprised to find an actual website by this name until I read the first sentence – 'You are not here by accident'. And that's when I began my life-changing journey with Steve and Barbara Rother and the group.

Lightworker, and most recently the LightMaster courses they offer, have changed my life in so many ways I can't even begin to list all of them. I feel like I've finally found my spiritual family here on Earth and I am overwhelmingly grateful for the gifts they have offered me. I feel such a strong connection to my LightMaster family, especially when we're working together energetically for the planet.

This book is a result of the LightMaster work I've been doing with this group for the last three years. We were asked, "What is your passion? If you were asked to speak to the other LightMasters about your passion, what would you say?" And that's when I began to compile and organize this information about my joy and passion, *Singing Crystals*.

I consider myself a life-long learner and bibliophile (avid reader). I also like to share what I'm learning and have been an intuitive healing facilitator and teacher for many years. I love to plant 'seeds' and empower others to self-heal. It's so much fun for me to watch as the person I'm working with grows and changes. And the best part is, with every sharing, I grow and change as well.

But my biggest love, the thing I would choose before all else, is spending time in Nature and harmonizing with Mother Earth. I consider this to be my raison d'être on planet Earth at this time.

Chapter 1: Beginnings

My first encounter with the 'wild' happened about 6 months after moving from Ontario to the south-eastern corner of beautiful British Columbia. We had been camping at one of the local lakes for the holiday weekend in May and had stopped at another smaller lake on the way home so that Carl, my new partner, could do a bit more fishing. I wanted to stretch my legs before the drive home and Carl let me out of our canoe at the bottom of a steep bank. I climbed the bank and that's when I met my first grizzly bear.

Luckily for me the bear was more interested in the garbage bin than in me or Carl's dog, Lucas. Lucas was a wolf-cross who had helped himself to a pound of butter from someone else's picnic table earlier that day. Because he wasn't feeling very well he didn't engage with the bear, which was probably a life-saver for me since dogs have a tendency to make bears very angry.

At this time, back in the 1980's, the Forestry department was still maintaining public campsites and providing open barrels for garbage. The bear was having a feast after the long-weekend campers had left the bin overflowing. I didn't even notice him until Lucas gave a strange bark, which I later learned was a dog's 'bear bark'. The grizzly jumped up a small tree to avoid Lucas and Lucas and I ran back down the bank where Carl met us with the canoe. He asked me about the size of the bear but I had nothing to compare it to since this was the first time that I had ever seen a bear in the wild. All I saw was a bum up a tree. The tree trunk was pretty small so I told Carl it must be a small bear, at which point he told me we had to watch for the mother. Carl had grown up in rural Quebec and had been caught between a momma bear and her cub when he was a boy. Though that episode had ended well, he had learned enough to be cautious about letting himself become caught in similar circumstances.

We had a few anxious moments while packing up the canoe. We had parked beside a small hill just a short distance away, and we couldn't see the campsite or the bear from where we were. After a weekend of fishing the canoe smelled like fish and we were worried that the bear would come to check out the tantalizing aroma. But we managed to finish with no problems. When we got into the car – a Toyota Corona – Carl said, "Let's go see this bear. He's probably still in the garbage and we should be able to get a good look".

As we approached the campsite the bear left the garbage bin and crossed the road right in front of us. It was a grizzly, with a large hump, and was bigger than our car! He was the most beautiful animal I had ever seen, with shiny, honey-brown fur. He stopped behind a few bushes so we were able to get a really good look at him.

Carl teased me for years about the 'small' bear, but hey, it was my first-ever bear and when all you see is a bum up a tree it's pretty hard to judge! Because he was insistent about coming back to the garbage bin at this campsite, within 3 weeks of our encounter this grizzly was trapped and relocated up north.

My next 'wild' encounter happened just a few weeks later. We were going camping and planned to explore the Kootenay – Palliser River area. As we pulled up to the old, wooden, one-lane bridge over the Kootenay River, we had to stop before crossing. In the middle of the bridge was a young deer, a buck, and we didn't want to scare him into jumping off and getting hurt. We got out of the car and to my surprise Carl started talking to him and walking slowly towards him. The deer, like many of our wild friends, liked the sound of Carl's voice and came right up to us. We got to spend a bit of time with him, petting and talking to him.

From that point on I was really hooked!! I was in love with this place I now called home. Our love for this area is the reason that Carl and I eventually created the Singing Crystal Network.

****

My connection to nature started early in my life. I grew up on the Great Lakes in southern Ontario. My father had a deep love of nature and I learned a lot from him during my childhood. We weren't allowed to play much in the house unless the weather was really nasty, so we spent most of our free time playing outdoors. In those days we weren't driven to school or activities by our parents. We walked or biked everywhere.

My early love for nature was also influenced by the TV programs I watched when I was young, especially the unique and entertaining nature programs that used to be produced by The Wonderful World of Disney. I also enjoyed shows like Gentle Ben, Grizzly Adams and Dr. Doolittle. I loved the main character's ability to interact with their wild and not-so-wild companions. I imagine that this is where my desire to connect to birds and animals originated. I also learned from watching these programs that *all life* deserves our respect and compassion.

I'm emotionally empathic and in hindsight, I can see how I've been affected by this my entire life. I believe that that's another reason I love being out in nature so much – it's where I find my peace and calm, away from the erratic emotions of humans. For the past few years though, I've become aware that I'm empathic with birds and animals as well. I feel the strong emotions, like fear and anxiety. I would suddenly feel a brief but intense fear after driving past a deer on the side of the road, even though we had been nowhere close to hitting it. I've felt the anxiety of a pair of adult Canada geese who were protecting six very young goslings and were startled when we suddenly appeared beside the creek where they were feeding.

But the best example I can give involves our dog, Beau. Beau loves to play with his ball in the current of the creek. One of his favourite games is to put his ball in the current and watch it float down the creek, while Carl uses his slingshot and tries to hit the ball with pebbles. On more than one occasion the ball has been lost in the current, which upsets Beau for the rest of our walk. I began to experience what felt like intense anxiety while watching this game, which really made no sense to me. After all, it was just a tennis ball and easily replaced. I finally realized that it wasn't anxiety but Beau's excitement that I was feeling.

I have always had an interest in energy flows, including but not limited to telepathy, healing energy, yoga and meditation journeys. My most impressive example of how telepathy works happened many years ago with Carl. He had gone to one of the local ski hills and late in the day I received a rather frantic phone call from one of his clients. They needed to speak to him before 5 pm and I knew Carl wouldn't be home in time to get the message. You have to understand this was years before cell phones were available, so I had no way to contact him except with a telepathic message. I sat down and imagined I was talking to him face-to-face. I kept the message simple: "Call me!" I waited 5 minutes, 10 minutes and at 15 minutes decided that he wasn't paying attention enough to get the message – and that's when the phone rang! Without even saying hello, the first breathless words out of his mouth were, "I got your message when I was at the top of the hill, but I had to ski down to the lodge to get to the phone." How's that for 'proof'?

I became quite ill during my 30's and 40's mostly due, I believe, to my intensifying sensitivity to the discordant and disruptive energies around me. I started to read books on how to clear my energy field and control my reactions more effectively. I have since learned many exercises and meditations to manage these feelings, though I still find myself reacting when things are particularly intense. One of the modalities that has helped immensely is Reiki. I became a Reiki Master in 2003 (Carl became a Reiki Master/Teacher and a Touch for Health therapist in 1999).

Since September of 2011, when I began to participate in the LightMaster program, the techniques I've been learning have enabled me to expand the ways in which I use the Singing Crystal Network. These skills, including harmonization and expansion, have enhanced my energy flow and affected everything that I do, including working with the network. Remember the geese with the six babies? I now know how to send out a calming energy and was able to settle things enough for them that they went about their business of watching over their feeding babies. Though the adults continued to keep a close eye on us, their anxiety was greatly lessened.

Since I moved to this area over 35 years ago, Carl and I have spent many hours out in the wilds of British Columbia. We have had so many amusing, heart-warming and exciting encounters that I have grown to love nature even more. Being in the wild, melding and harmonizing with the energy, becoming just another part of the landscape has enabled us to have so many unique experiences. When the invitation came to add healing, clearing and balance to this area, I jumped at the chance to use my energy to make a difference here.

Chapter 2: The Invitation

In the spring of 2004 I received a rather lengthy email inviting me to participate in an event called the Massive Medicine Wheel, set for May 8th 2004. This was to be a Blessing Ceremony for Mother Earth and was being held due to a flood of dreams and visions experienced by an Eastern Shoshone man named Bennie LeBeau. Mr. LeBeau lived high in the mountains of the Continental Divide and he was becoming distressed by the changes in the land and the animals in Yellowstone National Park. He believed that the energy of the Earth was out of balance due to many human activities such as mining, logging, vehicles, dams, transmission lines and indiscriminate development.

Mr. LeBeau felt it was time to reconnect the energy of the sacred sites and was looking for assistance to reactivate these sites. He also believed that the ley lines of the Earth could be adjusted with energy in the same way a human body can be adjusted with acupuncture.

The invitation was sent out for all races and traditions, since a healthy Earth is necessary to everyone's survival. There was to be no set ceremony. He asked only that people follow their hearts and use their intentions to bring balance, respect, gratitude and healing to their area of the planet. His intention was to use the ceremony to 're-set the basic tone or vibrational pattern of the West, and by extension, help re-attune the whole of the Earth'.

As I came to the end of the email and read the list of areas included in the approximately 600-mile radius of the Massive Medicine Wheel, both the Three Sisters (Banff, Alberta) and Lake Louise were mentioned as being two of the ceremonial points around the perimeter. That's when I realized that the Columbia Valley was included within the boundaries as well. At this point I knew I wanted to participate. Now all I had to do was to decide how I could be most effective.

For many years I had explored various traditions including Native American spirituality, Wicca, Celtic ritual and other earth-based belief systems. I understood and practiced the concepts of the sacred circle and the flow of energy that can be created with our intent. I read and learned from authors like Jamie Sams, Ted Andrews, Starhawk, and Scott Cunningham to name just a few.

For a while when I was working on my health issues, I attended an energy-healing circle run by two intuitive healers. During a visit to our house one day, one of them pointed out the presence of a vortex which was centered under our front deck, just outside of the northwest corner of our living room. When I asked her to explain, she just told me to stand in the centre of it. I immediately felt like I was coming down with the flu – a stuffy, spinning head and nausea were the most noticeable symptoms. (See the Chapter 3 for more information on vortexes.) For years we had been unknowingly stabilizing this vortex with a sacred circle we had created just inside the northwest corner of the living room.

Carl and I both love crystals and stones and our collection grew yearly. Carl was so interested that he bought and started using a stone tumbler/polisher. We now had an extensive collection of polished stones and crystals ready to be charged and programmed.

Putting It All Together:

I decided to use all of the elements I had available and my plan became to create a 'wheel within a wheel'. I charged up some crystals and stones in our sacred circle beside the vortex and then placed them in our abalone-shell, mirrored-bottomed pyramid to enhance their 'charge'. Carl and I programmed the crystals with Reiki and our intentions for clearing, healing, gratitude and peace. We then 'planted' them in a rough circle in various areas around the valley and up into the watersheds. And this is how the Singing Crystal Network began.

Chapter 3: Vortexes and Power Places

Vortexes:

So what exactly is a vortex and how do you find one? Vortexes appear everywhere in Nature and are not difficult to find if you know what you're looking for. A vortex is simply energy moving in a circular and/or spiral motion. Vortexes exist around many of Earth's sacred sites, but are not limited to these locations. All you have to do is to look into a creek or river to find many areas where the water is moving in a spiral or circle. Think of a tornado, water spout or hurricane – all are examples of vortex energy.

A vortex can circulate either clockwise or counter-clockwise. There are many opinions about what a particular direction means. I consider a vortex to be an 'energy amplifier', and as with everything else, I follow my instincts when deciding whether or not to work with a particular vortex. I always ask for permission and if it doesn't 'feel' right, I will leave it alone. I find though that most vortexes welcome our attention.

We've also seen 'double vortexes' or two vortexes side-by-side, one circulating clockwise and the one right beside it rotating counter-clockwise. These are most noticeable in a creek or river and they seem to create a very balanced energy.

We are also capable of creating vortexes of energy. I've experienced the raising of a 'cone of power', a vortex of healing energy that we created as part of a circle group. It was really interesting to feel the energy build and flow through us and around the circle, lifting up out of the circle and then release, as if by a signal, although one was not given. We projected this healing energy around the globe.

As I mentioned in Chapter 2, being in the middle of a vortex can feel uncomfortable to say the least. Some trigger physical 'symptoms' like stuffed sinuses, dizziness and nausea. It can feel like you're coming down with the flu. They can also cause sleepiness and make you feel drained of energy.

I used to think that Carl and I had to be a couple of the most boring people on the planet. When we had visitors over they would sit on our couch and fall asleep! At the time we had no idea that we had a vortex nearby but I now realize how much of an effect it had on everyone in the house. It also explained why we couldn't bring ourselves to sit in that area on our deck. Even if it was the only place for shade on a hot day, I would put my chair there and then soon find that I had unconsciously moved away from this particular spot, even if I ended up in the sun again. Once we set up the sacred circle in our living room, we no longer had guests snoring through the evening. The crystals in the circle helped to calm and stabilize the energy.

Another place where we have an annual close encounter with a vortex is in our timeshare unit in Fairmont Hot Springs. The Columbia Valley is riddled with hot springs and underground water flows which are ideal for vortex formation, and Fairmont is one of the more powerful of these areas. The first time we stayed at our timeshare was in November of 2002. I was exhausted after overdoing it at work and for days experienced flu-like symptoms. Every time I sat down to enjoy the fireplace in the living room, I felt nauseated, dizzy and stuffed up. But when we went out for our daily walk or when I went into our bedroom, I felt fine. We were both very inexperienced at the time, so it took us almost the entire week to figure out that the end of the couch where I liked to sit was in the middle of a vortex!

Now one of the first things we do when we arrive in our unit is move the couch over a couple of feet and place some crystals in the vortex to settle the energy. I often wonder how others who stay in that same unit feel while they are there. I know that we're not the only ones sensitive to these energies.

If you'd like to check your living area for vortex energy you can use a pendulum in each room to check for circular energy. Finding a vortex may explain why a certain area of your house or yard feels different or difficult to be around. If you're unfamiliar with how to use a pendulum, check out one of the many video tutorials on YouTube.

As it turns out, the first crystal we 'planted' as part of the Massive Medicine Wheel event in 2004, was at another vortex we visit on a regular basis. This is at one of our favourite spots along a creek very close to home. This is the place where I go to meditate, re-group and calm myself, and it's also the place where I do many of the energy exercises that I learn about through LightMaster. I have a beautiful spot under a tree about 3 metres from the centre of the vortex which is in the middle of the creek.

When we planted this first crystal under the tree, the surroundings looked different than they do today. Not only has the flow of the creek changed due to high water during spring run-off and ice jams changing the creek bed, but a few years after planting the crystal, large rocks were piled here by the local works department to strengthen the bank to prevent flooding along the creek. At first I felt heartbroken, like my 'sacred place' had been ruined. But I soon realized that not only had they buried the crystal so deeply it would probably never move from this spot during my lifetime, but the tree which I was so concerned about continued to grow and thrive. Usually if you cover the base of a tree in rocks it will die. I believe the healthiness of this tree to be one of the effects of the vortex.

This is also one of the first places where I actually 'saw' a vortex move. The first time it happened my first thought was that we were having an earthquake and my second thought was that I was ill or having a stroke or brain issue. The entire area around us seemed to be shimmering and rotating in a counter-clockwise direction, creating the feeling of motion sickness. I was sure when it stopped that the rocks around us would be in different positions but that wasn't the case. Carl and I looked at each other and realized that we had both seen and felt the same thing.

Since this first time both of us have seen this vortex and vortexes in other areas shimmer and move in the same way. We have had this happen in places where we didn't even realize that a vortex was present. It's always a welcome surprise and we appreciate the experience.

Seeing a vortex in motion can be a 'head-spinning' experience, but there are ways to stabilize the effect. Do you remember the 3D pictures that came out a few years ago? At first glance they looked like a random jumble of coloured patterns but if you defocused your eyes just right, a 3D image would appear in the pattern. I use this same defocusing technique to watch the movement of a vortex, instead of trying to focus on a particular spot.

A few years ago I started coming across information and a definition for people who work with vortexes like we do. We are known as 'vortex keepers'. I believe that Carl and I have had a 'contract' to work with these energies and the vortex at our house has become our connection point and amplifier for our entire Singing Crystal Network.

Do you need to have a vortex available in order to create your own Singing Crystal Network? Not at all! You can achieve similar results by finding and working with your very own Power Place.

Power Places:

So, what's the difference between a vortex and a Power Place? Power Places are everywhere on the planet and each individual person will have one or more areas where they feel connected to the Earth in a special way. Not all Power Places have vortexes nearby.

Both the Earth and Human Beings are electromagnetic in nature. A Power Place is a spot where you feel a strong connection with Mother Earth. People world-wide go to locations that are special to them and there are as many Power Places as there are people. Your connection to Mother Earth is a personal one and can be found by thinking about the places where you feel a bond or link to the planet. Trust your intuition, instincts and feelings when searching for your power place.

Where is your 'special' place? Is there a place in nature or in a park where you go to relax, re-group, calm yourself or meditate? Perhaps it's a place where you go for a time-out on a regular basis. Many Power Places are situated on or near water, whether it's a fountain, river, lake or the ocean.

Science has now proven that the connection between all things is very real. When we find and work with a Power Place, the energy generated affects and is recorded by everything in the area – trees, grass, stones etc. This draws even more energy to the area. Remember, not only can you add your energy to your Power Place, you can also 'draw' on the energy if you need a bit of a boost. That's why you feel so much better if you can get to your Power Place when you're having a difficult day.

I believe that one of the primary problems affecting the Earth right now is the disconnection between so much of humanity and the physical planet. It's time to put away the headphones and iPods, turn off your computers, cell phones and televisions, even if just for a short time and get out and experience what nature has to offer. How can we respect and protect the Earth if we have no physical ties to Her? When was the last time you felt the sun on your face, the wind in your hair, smelled the flowers, the grass and the trees? Do you know what water and snow smell like? Have you noticed the colours in the sunsets and sunrises? When was the last time you stopped and enjoyed the beauty of a rainbow or noticed the rainbow sparkles on the snow?

Your Power Place is a great place to acknowledge all of your gifts and give gratitude for everything that the Earth provides for you. All of us are catalysts for planetary change and we can enhance this by reconnecting and blessing our own particular 'special' place on the planet.

A Power Place is the perfect spot to plant an energized and programmed crystal or stone as part of your Singing Crystal network.

Chapter 4: Creating Sacred Circles

Sacred circles are ancient in origin and have been used by various cultures since the beginning of civilization. The circle is used to create sacred space, which defines the area used for ritual or connection and shuts out distractions. The circle is actually a sphere of energy rather than a circle. According to Wiccan beliefs the circle exists 'between the worlds' in a space where alternate realities meet.

Casting or creating a circle generates an energy form that allows us to raise 'power' or energy. This energy builds up the more you use and interact with the circle. The various parts of the circle are symbols of the interconnectedness of all life and represent the spiritual aspects of nature and the Earth.

The information provided below has been compiled by me from many traditions and earth-based philosophies. There is an enormous amount of material available if you'd like to do more of your own research in this area. My goal is for you to take the parts that resonate with your energy and use them in whatever way you feel inspired to do so. My 'vortex' circle represents the directions and the elements but is arranged in a way that my guidance tells me is the most effective for this particular purpose. Your personal intuition is the key to creating your own power circles.

There are seven directions contained within an energy circle, though not every direction will have a physical representation. The directions are East, South, West, North, Above, Below and Within. I activate the Above, Below and Within with my energy, which I will explain shortly.

The five elements included in the circle are Air, Fire, Water, Earth and Spirit. Again, Spirit is added when I activate the circle with my energy. You will provide the element of Spirit to your own circle. Each of the elements is connected to a specific direction within the circle.

East:

The East is the direction of greatest light and represents the light of wisdom, illumination and clarity. East is the doorway to alternative levels of awareness and assists with clear visualization. It helps us to let go of old habits and provides energy for healing and for transmuting negativity. East represents our psychic abilities and our power to 'know'.

The East is a masculine energy and is considered to be expansive and active. Its colour is the yellow of the sun, but East can also be represented by pale, airy colours. Its season is Spring and its time of day is the dawn. Eagle, who is free to soar and view all of creation, is linked to the East direction. The element associated with East is Air.

Within a sacred circle, Air can be symbolized by things like burning incense (the smoke is considered to be 'airy'), fresh flowers, feathers or any other symbol that denotes the theme of 'Air' for you.

South:

The South is the place where we connect with our innocence and inner child. It represents the spark of divinity contained within us and all living things. It teaches us to reconnect with our spirit of playfulness and to view life with the laughter and ease of a child. It can help to reopen our faith in ourselves and to trust in our original essence so that we can be more of who we came here to be. The South is the direction of purification and the evolution of our spirit.

The South is also a masculine energy and is considered to signify change, passion, and the destruction of negative habits. Fiery reds and oranges are the colours associated with the South. Its season is Summer and its time of day is noon. South is the direction for coyote and porcupine, who are both playful and curious. The element associated with South is Fire.

Symbols for fire are determined by whether your circle is indoors or outdoors. If indoors, use a candle, oil lamp or piece of lava rock. If outdoors, a fire can be used as long as you're in a safe location and the conditions are favourable. These are the most common ways to symbolize fire, but you can use anything that signifies 'Fire' for you.

West:

The West is the direction of introspection, goals and purification. It also represents our subconscious and our emotions. It is considered to be the 'looking within' place – the void where all of our answers reside. It is our connection to 'all our relations' and helps to expand our outlook on life. This is where we enter the stillness of sacred space to find our courage and the power to 'dare'. It's where we can go to formulate our plans for achieving our goals.

The West is a feminine, receptive energy which is constantly changing, like our emotions. The colours of the West are blue or black and its season is Autumn. Its time of day is twilight. West is represented by Bear, who retires to her cave to hibernate sometime near the end of Autumn. This symbolizes our ability to go to our personal 'cave' to 'digest' our ideas and creations, and to find answers to our questions. The element associated with West is Water.

Many items can be used to symbolize Water in your sacred circle. If your circle is outdoors, rain, snow or fog are suitable for your energy work. Or you can place your circle with a lake, pond, creek or river on the west side. For an indoor circle, a bowl or cup of water can be placed in the West position. If possible, collect some water from a natural source to use in your indoor circle. Another option is to collect a small bottle or jar of water from a creek, river or lake. Fill your cup or bowl with tap water and add a few drops of the 'natural' water. You can intend that this represent the 'waters of the world'.

Along with a small, indoor fountain, I also have a 550 gram 'river pebble' that I found in the elbow of a river, in the West of my circle. It's a wonderfully smooth, dove-grey stone that fills the palm of my hand. This is the stone I was holding when I first felt a flow of energy in my hands. Carl had taken his First Degree Reiki and had been trying to explain to me what this flow felt like. I had been trying different things to trigger this experience of flow and this stone gifted me with a small surge of energy one night while I was just holding it in my hand. Water can also be symbolized with representations of sea serpents, dolphins, fish or anything else that represents Water for you.

North:

The North is where we acknowledge our wisdom and gratitude and is considered to be the direction of abundance, prosperity and wealth. It is also the direction where we find the Goddess, the energy of the Earth Mother. This is the most powerful direction, that of the Mystery or unseen. The North Star is the centre around which the entire sky revolves. Here we find the power of listening to the Earth and all creatures who exist upon Her. Our wisdom is an inner knowing that can help to teach us the proper use of truth, forgiveness and humility. This is where we offer our prayers of thankfulness and gratitude.

The North is a feminine energy – nurturing, fruitful and stabilizing. The colours of the North are green or snowy white and its season is Winter. Its time of day is midnight and it is also connected to the New Moon. North is represented by the sacred White Buffalo, encouraging gratitude for lessons learned. Earth is the element associated with North.

In your sacred circle Earth can be represented by a bowl of salt or earth, crystals, or anything that signifies 'Earth' for you. Many years ago in a high school art class we were working with clay and our assignment was to create a likeness of the Venus of Willendorf. The original piece was made between 25,000 and 28,000 years ago and was found during an excavation near Willendorf, Austria in 1908. She has become my representation of the Goddess, and little did I know during that art class so many years ago, that my Venus would be with me and a part of my energy work for years in the future. She sits in the North of my vortex circle. There are many figurines that symbolize Goddess energy, so find one that resonates with you, if you'd like to include one in your sacred circle.

Spirit:

As mentioned above, Spirit is the 5th element within your circle. You bring this with you every time you interact with your sacred circle and your Singing Crystal Network. To activate this element it is important that you approach the building and activation of your circle with clear intent and that you're well grounded before starting your work. The simplest grounding exercise is as follows:

Create a place where you can be undisturbed and begin to bring your consciousness to the centre of your body. Take three deep breaths, equal in and out, and on the third breath stop breathing when half of the air has been expelled. Find your centre, which for most us is in the heart area. Breathe normally when you feel the need to oxygenate again.

Imagine that the centre of your being is full of light and run this light down through your body, down through your feet and use the light to grow your 'roots' from the bottom of your feet to the centre of the planet, whatever you imagine this to be. Once your light reaches the centre of the planet, bounce it back all the way up, back through your feet and body and out the top of your head. Send your beam of light to the centre of the Universe, whatever you imagine this to be. Once your light reaches the centre of the Universe, bounce it back down to join the downward stream of light in the centre of your being. You are now grounded with two flows of light, one up, one down and meeting in your centre. Allow your heart to glow with this light and expand this glow outward.

Intention is your most important tool when building and using your sacred circle and your Singing Crystal Network. Decide what you would like to accomplish with this energy and hold this in your mind as you're building your circle or working with your Network. Keep it simple. I like to send love and light. If you put too many parameters on your energy, you tie the hands of Spirit to doing only what you intended. Sending love and light allows Spirit to utilize the energy in the most effective way possible.

Above, Below and Within:

Above, Below and Within are also directions in a sacred circle but it can be a bit difficult to find or place representations of these energies in the appropriate places. The easiest way to activate these is by using your energy. Once you are grounded and have created your circle or whenever you want to activate it, stand over it and use either your right or left hand to move the energy over the circle. With my palm down I circle three times counter clockwise, then three times clockwise. I then lift my hand, palm up, towards the sky. Then push my hand, palm down, towards the Earth. I then bring my hand and place the palm on my heart centre for the within direction.

Our Vortex Circle:

For many years we created a sacred, directional, elemental circle every weekend on our living room floor. Then we adopted a puppy and a kitten and the floor was no longer an option. That's when we created a more permanent circle closer to the vortex. We still acknowledge the seven directions and have representations of the four elements but the arrangement is slightly different.

In our vortex circle there are two 10 cm quartz point crystals marking the North and East. In the South we have an amethyst cluster and in the West is the river pebble I mentioned above. Also included between these crystals are the following: another smaller amethyst cluster, a cluster of very small quartz crystals, a phantom crystal (a quartz crystal with inclusions), two Lemurian seed crystals, a large amethyst point, two seashells, three pairs of hematite magnets, feathers and my Goddess figurine. We also have a small fountain nearby, though it's too big to include in the circle itself.

As you can tell, our circle is based on crystal energy to help to settle the vortex. When we want to cleanse or activate crystals and stones for the Network, we temporarily add them to the circle to charge them up.

Putting Your Sacred Circle Together:

The first step to creating your own circle is to begin to collect the items and elements you want to include. I recommend that you make this a fun, creative and enjoyable experience. Children are naturals at energy work and this could be a pleasurable activity for the entire family. If you're unsure about where the directions lie, use a compass. Follow your own intuition and guidance to choose what will work best for you and for your intentions for your circle. There is no 'wrong' way to do this – just follow your heart and allow your playfulness to participate.

I find that with the changes in vibration and energy on the planet in recent years, long, drawn-out rituals for doing energy work are no longer necessary. The connection is made more easily now and being grounded allows you to hear your own guidance more clearly, especially with practice.

That being said I highly recommend that if this is the first time you've ever created a sacred circle, you take your time and really get into the spirit of each direction as you form your circle. Set aside some time when you will be undisturbed. Remember to ground yourself first. If you're creating your circle indoors, play some soft, inspiring music. If you're forming your circle outdoors, listen to the 'concert' that nature is playing for you at the time.

If you are creating your sacred circle in an outdoor space, choose one that will remain undisturbed by other people or birds and animals. If that's not possible, create a 'temporary' circle that you remove once finished with it for the day.

There are two very important elements that should be a part of every sacred circle creation. The first is your Gratitude. The second is your SMILE, so don't forget to include yours!

Chapter 5: Choosing Stones and Crystals

Now that you have created your sacred circle, it's time to start collecting the stones and crystals that you want to 'plant' in your Singing Crystal Network. If you've been a collector like Carl and I have been, you may already have some crystals or polished stones you'd like to use. If you're a beginner you can either collect your stones in nature or purchase them. Many businesses now have bins of inexpensive, polished stones that you can choose from.

For the purpose of your network, stones and crystals can be used interchangeably. Both are a form of piezoelectric energy and can be used to store and amplify any energy fed to them. When you add 'stress' to a crystal, in the form of energy, the crystal will emit its own individual energy frequency or vibration. This is why I use the term 'singing' crystals.

Have you even attended an event that included 'toning'? Imagine an entire auditorium of people all toning or humming together. Each individual adds their own unique tone or note and what I find the most interesting is that when it's time to stop, the entire group stops toning at once. No one tells everyone to stop – it just happens instantly. This is because toning harmonizes the entire group to a similar vibrational energy. In the same way, activating just one of your crystals can have a similar effect. It can trigger the other crystals in your network to vibrate and release their own unique tones.

Our ancestors had extensive knowledge of the power of stones and crystals. Tribal healers and shamans have used crystals for healing and divination for generations and information about their use can be found in the teachings of many cultures around the world. Caverns and chambers of crystals were used as healing chambers to promote healing in the mental, physical, emotional and spiritual bodies. Crystals can modify our subtle energy patterns to achieve harmony within the body.

In many native traditions, stones are considered to be record holders, collecting the energy and recording all that occurs in a particular area. Stones can be 'read' by those sensitive to their energies. We can connect to stones and crystals for healing, focus and clarity. They have an earthing influence and can help to dispel confusion and to reconnect us to the Earth, which calms us. On a spiritual level crystals can create profound shifts in our awareness.

It takes very little effort to program and release a crystal's energy. Energy follows thought, or in this case, your intention. If you project loving, calming, peaceful thoughts and intentions to a crystal, those particular vibrations are absorbed by and combined with the energy field of the stone. When you 'activate' your network, these intentions are released as electromagnetic energy, in the form of a vibration or tone. In other words, the crystals 'sing' in harmony.

Purchasing Stones and Crystals:

As mentioned, many retailers now sell polished stones. So how do you choose, when there are so many options available? The best criteria are your feelings and instincts. Which stones are you attracted to? Do you like the colour, feel and smoothness of the stone? Pendulums and muscle testing are other ways to determine if a stone is right for your energy. Or you can choose randomly, by letting the Universe decide which stone ends up in your hand.

If a stone feels 'funny' to you and you can't wait to put it down again or if you find yourself putting it back in the bin unconsciously, then that stone is not for you. If you can't bring yourself to put it down or you keep picking it back up again, you've found one you can resonate with.

Some crystals will wait for the right person and 'find' you. Recently I was looking for a gift to give to Carl for our 35th anniversary. According to the information I found on the internet, jade or coral was the gift of choice.

One store owner handed me a piece of Nephrite Jade and I knew immediately that this was what I was looking for and that it would resonate with Carl's energy. I told her I would like to purchase it, which is when she told me the following story. A few months prior a woman had come into the store specifically to buy a piece of Nephrite Jade. The owner knew she had a beautiful piece in the store, but looked everywhere she could think of and couldn't find it. She even checked the computer and couldn't find it there either. She assumed one of her employees must have sold it.

A few hours after the woman left the store, the owner found the piece of jade in one of the areas she had already checked (it was also back in her computer entries). She phoned the woman to tell her she'd found it, but the woman had already purchased one in another store.

This piece of Nephrite Jade remained in the store for months until I showed up to purchase it for Carl. The store owner and I both believe that it energetically 'hid' and waited until it had the opportunity to be connected with Carl's energy.

Cleansing:

The first thing to do when you get your new crystals home is to cleanse them. Even if you intend to use stones and crystals that have been in your possession for some time, it is still advisable to cleanse them prior to charging and programming them for your network.

There are a number of ways to cleanse a crystal. My suggestion is to use the one that is the most interesting and fun for you. If you live in an area that experiences cold winters, access to creeks and rivers can be limited to the warmer months and may not always be an option. Try a few different methods to determine which works the best for you.

Cleansing is important, so don't skip this step! Cleansing clears any negative energy and residual programming present in the crystal. Think about how many people have handled your stone before it came into your life. It can be affected by energy from the miner, buyer, polisher, importer, transporter, seller and anyone who has handled it in any way. Because of this, uncleansed crystals can have adverse effects and can trigger headaches or feelings of being unsettled, scattered or anxious.

My favourite way to cleanse crystals is by putting them in running water like a creek or river. Use caution – you don't want your new crystal floating down the creek in the current! Running tap water is also suitable for cleansing.

Another option is to fill a glass (not metal) bowl with water and add sea salt. Sea salt is inexpensive and can be purchased at most grocery stores. Make sure your stones are completely covered and soak for 24 hours. Rinse in running water.

Reiki or any other energy-healing modality can be used as well. Run your energy into the stone with the intention that it be cleared of any energy that isn't yours.

Putting your stones outside to soak up sunlight or to be exposed to the full or new moon is also effective. I like to think of exposing crystals to the new moon as filling them with starlight. Sunlight and moonlight are also good for charging your stones, once cleansing is complete.

Charging:

Crystals can be compared to batteries – they can become depleted with use and have to be re-charged periodically. Once cleared, I like to put my stones in my crystal circle and have them charged not only by the other crystals in the circle, but also by the vortex. We have a small pyramid made out of abalone shell. One side opens and the bottom is mirrored. I store the charged crystals here until I'm ready to take them out and plant them. Sometimes I just keep them in the crystal circle itself.

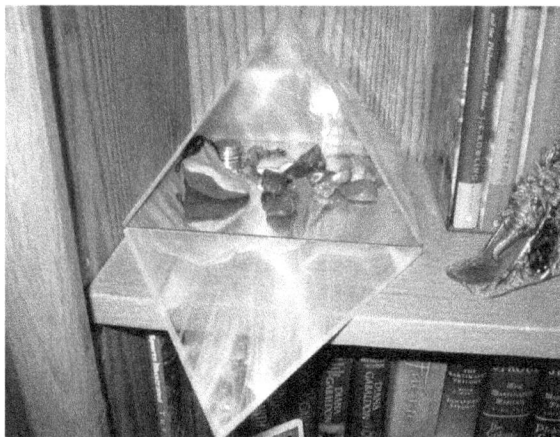

You can charge crystals by placing them out in sunlight, moonlight and starlight or by putting them outside during storms. I love to put my crystals out on the 'power' days, like solstices and equinoxes.

You can also place smaller stones and crystals on larger crystal clusters to charge them.

Programming:

Remember, energy follows thought. I recommend that you take some time to become clear about what kind of energy you want your crystal to emit. Once you have a clear intention for your stone, hold the crystal in your hand and run your intention from your heart, through your arms and fingers and into the crystal. Keep your intentions as simple as possible. If you put too many parameters on your programming, spirit may not be able to use the energy to its best advantage. If in doubt or if you don't have a specific purpose in mind, simply program it with light and love.

I also like to intend that the stone or crystal spread its energy once planted. Like ripples from pebbles thrown in a pond, the energy spreads and eventually overlaps with the energy fields of other stones I've planted in the area.

You may feel the stone warming up or vibrating. It doesn't take long to program a stone and you'll know intuitively when the programming is complete. Use each stone or crystal for a singular purpose – no multi-tasking! In other words, you will program each stone with gratitude and for the purpose of healing, cleansing and protecting the Earth (or whatever your intention is). You would not use the same stone for sending healing to your Aunt Sophie, or for any other goal.

The programming will be effective until the crystal is cleansed, cleared and programmed for another purpose. I consider the stones I've planted to be permanently programmed, since I have no intentions of digging them up and using them for something else.

Remember, you are the interface with this subtle network of energy. It's your energy and intention that will keep the energy of your network flowing.

Your next step will be deciding where you want plant your cleansed, charged and programmed stones.

Chapter 6: Creating Your Network

When I created a 'circle within a circle' as part of the Massive Medicine Wheel event, I had to determine where exactly I wanted to 'plant' these crystals. I decided the first one should be really special and close by. As mentioned, I ended up burying a beautiful quartz crystal point under my favourite tree at my meditation spot down by the creek not far from home. I spend quite a lot of time here doing energy and healing work, so it seemed like the perfect place to begin.

For the remainder of this first 'planting', I chose areas that would form a rough circle around town. Carl and I spent about a week before the Massive Medicine Wheel event travelling around to these areas and planting our stones. On the day of the event we concentrated on connecting all of the stones we had planted, not only to our sacred circle which is next to our vortex, but also to each other. This was the beginning of our Singing Crystal network, though we didn't realize it at the time.

The problem was I didn't want to stop! I kept coming up with more areas that could use some help and healing. We had enjoyed the event so much that we were interested in continuing to plant areas that were not included in the original circle. Whenever we would go out on one of our 'bush' trips, I would have a pocket full of cleansed and charged stones, which we would program and plant wherever we were guided to enhance the energy. Each of these places was then added to the network using my intention and the energy of the sacred circle.

Please note: you don't have to travel long distances or hike deeply into the backcountry to do this work, though you can if you're so guided. Most of our network is accessible by car though some areas can only be reached by 4-wheel drive. We do have some stones placed in areas that we've had to hike to, but that's because we love the hike.

The one commonality I have noticed in our choice of locations is that we have instinctively placed many of our crystals in or near a source of water. After reading about the work of Dr. Masaru Emoto, I now understand why. If you are unfamiliar with Dr. Emoto's work, I recommend you do a bit of research into his experiments detailing the effects of our emotional energy on water. Check the bibliography for the titles of two of his most popular books. His work is also featured in the DVD *What the Bleep Do We Know*, previously mentioned.

Dr. Emoto's work involved collecting water samples from various sources, some natural, some not, and freezing and photographing the individual crystals as they formed. Water from pure, natural sources created beautiful, evenly-formed crystals, while water from polluted sources (including the tap water in many cities) often wouldn't form crystals at all.

He also did experiments with putting pure water in jars and either taping short messages to the jar or playing various forms of music in the room. The water exposed to messages like 'I hate you' or 'Fool' or exposed to heavy metal music formed shapeless, blobby non-crystals, while water exposed to messages like 'I love you' or 'Love and Gratitude' or to classical music, formed beautiful, even crystals.

So, what does all of this mean? Could it be that water can be 'programmed' like crystals? If water has the ability to copy and memorize information, or energy, that means our emotions and intentions can have an effect on the health of our water. Dr. Emoto's experiments showed that water responds to positive words and emotions with beautiful crystals. What if we started to use our Singing Crystal Networks to send healing and cleansing to our water sources?

One of my favourite stories from one of Dr. Emoto's books involved a group of 350 people who met early one morning at heavily polluted Lake Biwa in Japan. Led by a Master, this group used the power of words (ie: vibration) with the intention of clearing this beautiful lake. Noticeable effects were reported by the local media within a month.

A number of our stones and crystals are sitting in the bottom of many of the small lakes in our area. In some lakes we've placed only one; in others we may have dropped two or three stones into the water at various locations around the lake. There was no 'logic' involved – I would just go with my instincts while on the lake in our canoe and place as many as seemed to be required by this particular location. Again, most of the crystals were programmed with peace, clearing (if necessary), love, light and gratitude. According to many current sources the vibration of gratitude is as powerful as the vibration of love, so be sure to include it with every stone you program.

We've also 'dropped' many crystals off the edges of canyons or high banks besides creeks, rivers and adjacent to the extensive wetlands that are found in the Columbia River valley. Be cautious about what kind of stone you toss over a bank. Delicate crystals may shatter if used in this way so with this method it is better if you use only polished stones.

In one area we were guided to create a small sacred circle marking the four directions. We personally call this area 'Top of the World' though this is not its official name and is not to be confused with the provincial park of that name. We love to hike and picnic in this spot – there's a 360 degree view of the mountains at the 'top', available due to an intense forest fire in the area in 1994. We placed the circle as part of the healing of the area, adding our 'spirit' every time we visit. We are really starting to notice the healthy growth of the new trees. So much so, that we're slowly losing our 360 degree view!

This area and a few others do not seem to be connected to a nearby water source but if you consider the rain and snow that fall and filter through the ground to join the ground-water, water is still very much involved.

Another thing I've learned during my years of energy work is something that I consider every time I intend to plant a new area. I learned this during the horrific Gulf of Mexico oil spill in April of 2010. Immediately, Lightworkers from around the globe, Carl and myself included, started pouring Light and a quick resolution to the situation into the Gulf. But for weeks nothing seemed to happen.

It was extremely confusing – until I received an email explaining the problem. There was so much negativity in the form of anger, fear and hatred aimed at the oil wells in the Gulf and also at the people who were held responsible for the leak, that there was nowhere for the Light and healing to go. It was like trying to pour water into an already full glass.

What we were asked to do was to imagine many 'pagoda bells' over the Gulf, ringing and siphoning off the negative energy. I 'saw' so many bells over the Gulf I wondered if everyone living around the area experienced ringing ears! Once the negativity was cleared, it was possible for the Light to go to work and within a week not only was the well successfully capped, but scientists started to discover several new-to-science species of microbes that were 'eating' the methane gas and oil and converting them to harmless elements.

If you're working with a heavily polluted or overused area, you may want to consider ringing a few bells over the area before you do your actual planting. Use your intention to place them over the area and set them to ring for a specified amount of time – 24 hours should be sufficient but use your own instincts.

Water is a necessity for all of life on Earth and is the life-force of nature. We can't exist without it, yet our sources of clean, drinkable water are becoming more contaminated with each passing day. Every being on the planet needs to have an abundance of clean water and *we can make a difference!*

Not only can you learn about the water conservation efforts in your area but now you can use your energy and intention to effect change. Remember Gratitude? Do you express your gratitude for having clean running water, a hot shower in the morning or water for your garden and access to clean lakes for recreational purposes? Your words of gratitude have vibrational frequencies which have an effect that is only beginning to be understood.

During the summer of 2013, I was once again hearing and reading about the radioactive contamination still pouring into the Pacific Ocean from the nuclear plants that were damaged during the tsunami in Japan. I started to wonder about sending healing and clearing from my meditation spot, down the creek and into the Columbia River, which exits into the Pacific between Washington and Oregon States in the US. Working consistently in an area has a cumulative effect, so why couldn't I just continue to add more clearing and healing and eventually have it reach the affected areas? I started to do a bit of research on the Columbia River and that's when I realized the problem was closer to home than I originally thought.

Chapter 7: Expansion

The Columbia River is the largest river in the Pacific Northwest region of North America. It has been used for transportation since ancient times and is by volume the fourth largest river in the United States. The drainage basin of the river is roughly the size of France and includes seven US states, plus British Columbia, Canada.

The headwater of the river is Columbia Lake, located approximately 40 kilometres from Invermere where we live. From the lake the river flows north, adjacent to an extensive series of wetlands. It eventually turns south, then west and ends up in the Pacific Ocean, approximately 2000 kilometres or 1243 miles from its beginning. There are 14 hydroelectric dams on the main river, used for power, irrigation and flood control.

As I began the research for this book, I remembered a co-worker many years ago telling me about a man who swam the Columbia in an effort to bring awareness to the problems facing the river. His name is Christopher D. Swain and in 2002 he spent 165 days swimming the entire length of the river, from Columbia Lake to the Pacific Ocean.

When Mr. Swain summarized his experience, he said that the last mouthful of clean water he took was in Columbia Lake. Once he entered the river system, he was exposed to herbicides from golf courses, pesticides from fruit orchards and municipal and raw sewage. But the worst and most worrying stretch was the area around Hanford, Washington, where the river is contaminated with neurotoxic poisons.

The Hanford Nuclear Facility is located only five miles from the Columbia River and is considered to be the most contaminated nuclear site in the US. For decades, plutonium for nuclear weapons was produced at the Hanford site. Now the site is used as a storage facility for nuclear waste. During a routine inspection in June of 2013, it was discovered that some of the underground tanks are beginning to leak, which is adding even more radioactive material to the area.

When Mr. Swain was asked why he would undertake such an enormous project and expose himself to all the toxins present in the water, he said he did it because he loved the river and all it supports, and he swam it in an effort to bring awareness to the problems it's facing.

One of the things that I've learned from the LightMaster classes I've been taking is to expand and utilize my energy for the benefit of the planet. As mentioned, I do many of these exercises at my meditation spot down by the creek. This creek flows into the Columbia River about 2 kilometres away from where I do this energy work.

Strangely, we have never been guided to plant stones in Columbia Lake, Lake Windermere or in the Columbia River itself, at least not yet. We do spend time every November working with the energy of the river not far from where it exits and begins its journey north from Columbia Lake. The river is so narrow here you could walk across it. By the time it reaches the Pacific it is almost 7 kilometres wide!

Every November when we spend time in Fairmont Hot Springs, we hike from our timeshare unit to the river and spend time at a vortex located there. The vortex was 'shown' to us one year when ice was beginning to form on the river. In one spot there was a large, free-floating, circular patch of ice that was rotating quite rapidly in a clockwise direction. We love the energy in this place and make a point of 'working' here at least two or three times during the week we're in the area.

I've connected both the vortex in the river and the vortex in our timeshare unit energetically to the vortex at our house and subsequently to our sacred circle and the entire Singing Crystal Network. The point I'm making here is that it's not necessary to always be physically present in order to work with your vortexes and power places. Once you've established and grounded your energy in a particular location, it's possible to activate and include this site in all of your energy work. All it takes is your focus and intention to include them. Imagine what it feels like to be physically present in this spot and connect *that* energy to your network.

As I continue to do my LightMaster exercises at the creek, I've decided to expand this to include extra time spent focusing on cleansing and healing the Columbia River. Since energy work is cumulative, I've been concentrating on sending my love, gratitude and Reiki healing down the creek to the river. I intend it to expand and spread healing energy into the surrounding wetlands, as well as sending it down the river system and out into the Pacific Ocean.

The wetlands are not only home to hundreds of different species, they also act like a giant, filtering sponge. They help to regulate the water systems in the valley by processing and absorbing much of the yearly run-off we get from melting snow in the mountains. During years of drought, they continue to hold water and help to maintain a balance.

Though we haven't 'planted' the river itself, almost all of the crystals we have placed do involve the river. The lakes, creeks and areas we work with are all a part of the Columbia River watershed. All of the energy we generate in these areas ends up flowing both up and down the Columbia River.

It seems like every time we foul our water in some gross way, science discovers another way in which Mother Nature helps out with the cleanup. From the oil- and methane-eating bacteria in the Gulf of Mexico, to the discovery of microbes that actually seek out and eat uranium and plutonium from the leaking reactors in Japan, who knows what scientists will discover next.

We need to do everything in our power to prevent more of these disasters, but we can also help energetically with the aftermath of these incidents. Anyone who knows Reiki understands the principles of distance healing and this energy can be used for the planet, as well as for individuals.

Considering the work of Dr. Emoto, I believe we can have a positive and healing impact on water molecules. I encourage you to find ways to help clean and clear the sources of water near you. Together we can make a huge difference on this planet we call home.

Chapter 8: Crystal Visions

As I write this, it's spring and the ice on the wetlands is beginning to melt. This is the time of year when, if we time it correctly, we get to see the 'spring social'. As the ice begins to recede from the edges and thin in the larger areas, eagles, both bald and golden, start to congregate on the ice near the open water. We will see a few different groups of 15 to 20 eagles, along with ravens, crows and magpies. Occasionally, a few of them will leave one group and join another. I always think of this as a social gathering of these birds after a long winter apart.

We see swans arriving daily on the river as they follow the melting ice north to their nesting grounds. The red-winged blackbirds and mountain bluebirds are back and soon the hummingbirds will arrive. It won't be long before we'll have to be more cautious when we're out and about – bears will be waking up hungry after a long, cold winter.

I encourage you to always be respectful and cautious when you're out setting up or working with your power places and network. There are areas that we won't go to at certain times of the year. Spring is nesting season on the wetlands and if we do visit we leave Beau at home and stay away from the edges where ducks may be nesting or watching over their feeding young ones. As mentioned, bears are waking up hungry and it's a good time to avoid those areas. A few days ago we had a very unexpected encounter with a moose in an area where we've never seen any sign of them before.

The fall is again a time where we choose our outings more carefully. Though our bear encounters have always been benign, we don't invite trouble by deliberately putting ourselves in harm's way. So, be aware of your surroundings at all times. Remember, it's not your 'right' to go anywhere you choose, anytime you choose. We share this planet and all are entitled to their 'space' at various times of the year.

Please show respect for the earth and for all of her inhabitants. Avoid sensitive areas when necessary and pick up any garbage you see. Continue to learn and grow yourself, as every shift in vibration you experience will impact your entire network. And always remember, your spirit shines brighter than any crystal!

One way to make this even more fun and enjoyable is to imagine your energy going out to your network in the form of 'fairy dust'. My 'fairy dust' can change in any way I desire, from tiny, sparkling white lights to rainbow sprinkles. It's easy for me to imagine this fairy dust travelling both up and down the creeks and rivers and travelling and spreading into the Pacific Ocean.

****

As I contemplate how I would like the information in this book to be used, I find myself dreaming about a 'collective' of Singing Crystal Networks. We now know that we really are all connected and we also know the effects of distance healing energies. I see no reason why we can't use these same principles to connect our networks together. If I imagine a series of Singing Crystal Networks, I 'see' all of our planted crystals as points of light, with lines of energy connecting the entire group. As the 'glow' from each crystal and network continues to spread, eventually this glow could cover and surround the entire planet. That means that whenever you want to utilize the network to send healing, peace or love, you can connect with the energy of the entire group of networks, not just your own.

It has crossed my mind that some of you may be concerned about the networks being used for 'negative' purposes. I'd like to share an image given to me by one of my teachers. Imagine you have two rooms, one fully light and one completely dark. There is a closed door between these two rooms. What happens when you open the door? Does the darkness enter and overtake the lighted room? No! (That would be creepy!) The light *always* enters the dark room. The 'dark' is nothing more than the absence of light.

In the same way, a network set up with the intentions of healing, love, joy, peace and gratitude cannot be contaminated with so-called negative or dark energies. The 'dark' is of a lower vibration and will not be able to harmonize with or influence the higher vibration of a 'light' network. Remember, your *intention* is the key.

Do I believe that my efforts with the Singing Crystal Network will magically heal all of the damage that has been inflicted on our planet? Of course not! But I do believe that every one of us can do our own small part to begin the shift in attitude and vibration that will help to assist the Earth Mother to achieve her balance once again.

Though we are a 'water' world, our water supply is in trouble. We either have too much, too little or it's too dirty and polluted. This is becoming more and more of an issue and we can make a difference. I'd like to conclude with a quotation from *The Hidden Messages in Water* by Dr. Masaru Emoto: "Wouldn't it be wonderful if we could cover the world in the most beautiful of water crystals?"[1]

---

[1] Dr. Masaru Emoto, The Hidden Messages in Water (Oregon, Beyond Words Publishing, 2004), 156

Connecting

If you are interested in connecting your Singing Crystal Network to our network here in the Columbia Valley, there are a couple of ways to achieve this. If you have your Second or Third Degree in Reiki, or another energy healing modality that utilizes distance work, you may already know about energy transfer over distance. The same technique can be used for connection. Find Invermere, British Columbia, Canada on a map and 'send' your intention to connect your power place or sacred circle energetically to our sacred circle. You can use the photo in Chapter 4, Creating Sacred Circles, to help you connect.

If you are unfamiliar with energy 'sending' you can contact me at linda2143@hotmail.com and I will be happy to set up the connection for you. All I will need from you is your location, but if you'd like to share, I'd love to read your stories about setting up your circles and networks.

If you don't have your Reiki attunements and would like to pursue this, there are many, many Reiki Masters and teachers available. Check the bulletin boards at wellness centres or health food stores to find someone in your area. It's inexpensive, quick and easy for *anyone* to learn.

Carl has recently been experimenting with the effectiveness of doing Reiki attunements over the internet, using a Skype connection. He tried this with the help of some locals, so he could meet with them in person afterwards to test how effective it was. The results have been better than we expected. If you are interested in receiving your attunements in this way, please email me at the address above.

With Gratitude

None of this would have been possible without the support and encouragement from my family and friends.

With heartfelt gratitude to the love of my life, Carl, for supporting and accompanying me on this journey. I never would have done all of this without you. To Beau and Tino for the love, laughs and hugs – you keep me en-light-ened up!

To Steve and Barbara, Austin, Meg, Judith and all of the Lightworker staff for making the Lightworker and LightMaster information so easily accessible and affordable, and for giving me a new life purpose and a safe place to spread my wings.

To the group, including Elrah, eM, and the Keeper of Time for your teachings and knowledge and for showing me ways to use this electromagnetic creation machine I inhabit, for the betterment of Gaia and all who dwell on Her.

To my proof readers, Carl, Annik and Denise – thank you. And a big thanks to Sharon for sharing your expert advice on the field of self-publishing with me.

And lastly, to my guides, angels and my 'entourage' for your patience, encouragement and healing when things seem so difficult for me. My intention is to keep you cheering!

Bibliography

Andrews, Ted, *Dream Alchemy*, St. Paul, MN, Llewellyn Publications, 1991

Cunningham, Scott, *Earth Power*, St. Paul, MN, Llewellyn Publications, 1992

Dyer, Dr. Wayne, *The Power of Intention*, Carlsbad, USA, Hay House, Inc., 2004

Emoto, Dr. Masaru, *The True Power of Water*, Oregon, Beyond Words Publishing, 2005

Emoto, Dr. Masaru, *The Hidden Messages in Water*, Oregon, Beyond Words Publishing, 2004

Harold, Edmund, *Focus on Crystals*, Toronto, Random House, 1987

Lilly, Sue, *Crystal Decoder*, London, Quarto Publishing, 2001

Melody, *Love Is In The Earth*, Colorado, USA, Earth-Love Publishing House, 1995

Sams, Jamie, *Sacred Path Cards*, New York, Harper Collins Publishers, 1990

Starhawk, *Spiral Dance*, New York, Harper Collins Publishers, 1989

Slade, Paddy, *Encyclopedia of White Magic*, London, The Hamlyn Publishing Group Ltd., 1990

www.ingramcontent.com/pod-product-compliance
Lightning Source LLC
Chambersburg PA
CBHW031332040426
42443CB00005B/313